IN SPIRIT AND IN TRUTH

THE POWER OF
NEW TESTAMENT
PRAISE AND WORSHIP

IN SPIRIT AND IN TRUTH

THE POWER OF
NEW TESTAMENT
PRAISE AND WORSHIP

by
RayGene Wilson

Harrison House
Tulsa, Oklahoma

Unless otherwise indicated, all Scripture quotations are taken from the *King James Version* of the Bible.

Some Scripture quotations are taken from *The Amplified Bible* (AMP). *The Amplified Bible, Old Testament* copyright © 1965, 1987 by The Zondervan Corporation. *The Amplified New Testament*, copyright © 1954, 1958, 1987 by The Lockman Foundation. Used by permission.

Some Scripture quotations are taken from *The New Testament: An Expanded Translation* by Kenneth S. Wuest. Copyright © 1961 William B. Eerdmans Publishing Co., Grand Rapids, Michigan.

In Spirit and In Truth
The Power of New Testament Praise and Worship
ISBN 1-57794-052-0
Copyright © 1997 by RayGene Wilson
RayGene Wilson Ministries
P. O. Box 4779
Tulsa, Oklahoma 74159

Published by Harrison House, Inc.
P. O. Box 35035
Tulsa, Oklahoma 74153

SPECIAL THANKS TO...

Beth, the love of my life and my best friend! I couldn't have done this without you. Thanks for your inspiration, your support, and always encouraging me to go for all that God has for me. I sure found a good thing when I found you! I love you with all my heart.

CONTENTS

CONTENTS

FOREWORD

Since Gloria and I have been in the ministry, we have enjoyed watching other ministries grow. It has been a real joy for us to have a part in someone's growth as a minister.

Over the last several years, we have watched RayGene Wilson grow and develop in the ministry. I once told Gloria, "You better watch that one. That kid's got fire in his eyes!" Recently, God began to show me some things that He is doing through RayGene's ministry. The Bible tells us how Philip was ordained first into the ministry of helps, then later he grew into the ministry of evangelism and was called "Philip the evangelist." He had grown from one place of ministry to another.

It's very interesting to see God develop a ministry and then to watch it grow and produce fruit. Through the years we have watched RayGene's ministry grow. We have seen the Spirit of God use him in the ministry of helps and develop him into an area of prophetic utterance in his music. It has been outstanding to watch the growth of this ministry. He has become one of the most powerful ministers of the gospel, in both preaching and singing, who travels the world today. By being around him, we have seen his hunger for God and what he is doing for the kingdom of God.

I say all of this not to give RayGene praise, because he doesn't require it, but because I want you, the reader, to receive from the Spirit of God through the anointing He has placed on RayGene's life and ministry.

Kenneth Copeland
Fort Worth, Texas

FROM THE AUTHOR

None of the writing in this book is original. Much of it dates back thousands of years; some of it came in the last few months. I received a lot of the material from my own study time in the Word and ministering to the Lord, and I received much at the feet of other ministers. I have been in a unique position to have had the opportunity to be associated with ministers like Kenneth Hagin, Kenneth Copeland, Mark Brazee, and Anne Durant. I listen to other ministers as well, but while studying the subject of praise and worship I fed mostly on their material. The spiritual deposits they have made into my life are immeasurable.

I wrote this book because I believe one of the most important things for the Body of Christ to know is how to create an atmosphere for God to move through praise and worship. There have been many things prophesied and written in the Word of God that have yet to come to pass. If we are going to see them come to pass, we are going to have to be in line with the Word of God. We are going to have to study the Word and find out God's plan for New Testament worshippers — not someone's idea of what praise and worship is, but what the Bible says it is. God doesn't bless man's plans; He blesses His plans.

"In Spirit" in the book is referring to being "in the Spirit." That's the way New Testament believers are to live our lives. "In Truth" of course is referring to the "Word of God." Jesus said in John 17:17, **Sanctify them through thy truth: thy word**

is truth. He also said in John 4:23, **But the hour cometh, and now is, when true worshippers shall worship the father in spirit and in truth: for the Father seeketh such to worship him.** If He is seeking true worshippers today, I want Him to find me! The fact that he said "true worshippers" implies there can be "false worshippers." This book talks about worshipping in spirit and in truth, the potential power that is made available to the Body of Christ and how to activate that power.

IN SPIRIT AND IN TRUTH

THE POWER OF
NEW TESTAMENT
PRAISE AND WORSHIP

CHAPTER 1

❁

NEW TESTAMENT WORSHIP

CHAPTER 1

❀

NEW TESTAMENT WORSHIP

As New Testament believers, everything we teach and preach and do should line up with the Word of God in light of the New Testament.

When it comes to healing, we are quick to quote 1 Peter 2:24:

> **Who his own self bare our sins in his own body on the tree, that we, being dead to sins, should live unto righteousness: by whose stripes ye were healed.**

When it comes to salvation, we speak Romans 10:9:

> **That if thou shalt confess with thy mouth the Lord Jesus, and shalt believe in thine heart that God hath raised him from the dead, thou shalt be saved.**

When we talk about being filled with the Spirit, we quote Acts 2:4:

> **And they were all filled with the Holy Ghost, and began to speak with other tongues, as the Spirit gave them utterance.**

When teaching on faith, we always go to Mark 11:23, where Jesus said:

> **For verily I say unto you, That whosoever shall say unto this mountain, Be thou removed, and be thou cast into the sea; and shall not doubt in his heart, but shall believe that those things**

which he saith shall come to pass; he shall have whatsoever he saith.

But then when it comes to praise and worship, we go back to the Old Testament!

Why is this?

We are sticklers for the Word of God in every area, and there is nothing wrong with using Old Testament Scriptures, but we have to interpret the Old Testament in light of the New Testament. If we are going to teach on any subject, no matter what that subject may be, we must have New Testament Scripture to back it up.

I have attended praise and worship conferences from coast to coast, but in such gatherings I have seldom heard anyone teach from the New Testament.

Why is it that we always go back to the Old Testament on the subject of praise and worship?

After asking this question, here are the two most common answers I have received: "We don't think there is a difference between the New and the Old," or "We don't think there is much about this subject in the New Testament."

In our study we are going to find that there *is* a difference between the New Testament and the Old, and we will see what the New Testament has to say about praise and worship.

KEY NEW TESTAMENT SCRIPTURE:

❀

THE WOMAN AT THE WELL

The woman saith unto him (Jesus), Sir, I perceive that thou art a prophet.

Our fathers worshipped in this mountain; and

ye say, that in Jerusalem is the place where men ought to worship.

Jesus saith unto her, Woman, believe me, the hour cometh, when ye shall neither in this mountain, nor yet at Jerusalem, worship the Father.

Ye worship ye know not what: we know what we worship; for salvation is of the Jews.

But the hour cometh, and now is, when the true worshippers shall worship the Father in spirit and in truth: for the Father seeketh such to worship him.

God is a Spirit: and they that worship him must worship him *in spirit and in truth* (italics added for emphasis).

John 4:19-24

This is, without a doubt, the key passage of New Testament Scripture on the subject of worship. Let's break it down now and discover what it says.

Earlier in this chapter from John's gospel, when Jesus was passing through Samaria, He stopped at Jacob's well for a drink of water. There, He asked a Samaritan woman for a drink. Dake's study Bible brings out some interesting points that will help us to understand the culture and the time in which these people were living[1]:

...Jewish etiquette and the Talmud [forbad] rabbis to converse with women in public or to instruct them in the Law. [No rabbi could] even converse with his wife, sister or daughter in public or in the streets.

The woman herself said to Jesus in John 4:9:

How is it that thou, being a Jew, askest drink of me, which am a woman of Samaria? for the Jews have no dealings with the Samaritans.

GOING AGAINST RELIGIOUS TRADITION

Jesus was good at going against religious tradition. He healed on the Sabbath. He ate with sinners. Now we find Him talking with a woman in public about spiritual matters. And it was not just the fact that He was speaking with a woman, but with a *Samaritan* woman as well! This was not accepted in their day because of the racial differences between the Jews and the Samaritans.

WHERE TO WORSHIP?

Besides the racial differences between the Jews and the Samaritans, there was a difference in where they worshipped. This was the key issue that separated them.

When the woman said in John 4:20, **Our fathers worshipped in this mountain**, she was talking about Mount Gerizim. That was where God's people worshipped in the first five books of the Old Testament and where the Samaritans still worshipped.

She continued in John 4:20, saying, **...and ye say, that in Jerusalem is the place where men ought to worship.** She was not talking here about Jesus Himself, but was referring to the Jews. The Jews worshipped in Jerusalem after the temple was built, and the glory of God appeared there. Every Jewish male who was thirty years old or older had to go to Jerusalem at least once a year and present himself before God at the temple.

WHO WAS RIGHT?

Jesus was reading that woman's mail when He told her in verse 18 that she had had five husbands and that the man she was with at that time was not one of them! So it didn't take long for her to figure out that Jesus was a prophet.

Then she decided to ask Him a question, the most important question of the day: Who was right?

This is what she was asking Him in John 4:20 when she said:

> **Our fathers worshipped in this mountain; and ye say, that in Jerusalem is the place where men ought to worship.**

So, who *was* right?

NEITHER ONE

Jesus answered her in verse 21 by saying that neither one was right. He said:

> **Woman, believe me, the hour cometh, when ye shall *neither* in this mountain, *nor* yet at Jerusalem, worship the Father.**

He continued in verse 23 to say:

> **But the hour cometh, and now is....**

This marks the difference between Old Testament worship and New Testament worship. This Scripture — John 4:23 — was the turning point. Jesus was referring here to the church age, the dispensation of the Holy Ghost.

Thank God, that is where we are today!

Now the emphasis has been taken off a *geographic location* and has been put on a *spiritual location*.

FROM THE OLD TO THE NEW

Jesus talked then about worshipping in the Spirit:

But the hour cometh, and now is, when the true worshippers shall worship the Father in spirit and in truth: for the Father seeketh such to worship him.

> **God is a Spirit: and they that worship him**
> **must worship him in spirit and in truth.**
>
> John 4:23,24

This was something brand-new to the people of that day. They couldn't do this under the Old Covenant. They didn't have God's Spirit living inside them the way believers do today. That's why they had to go to the temple at Jerusalem — where the Spirit of God dwelt, where the presence of God was shut up. Only kings, priests and prophets had the Spirit of God *upon* them, and no one had the Spirit of God *within* them!

In the Old Covenant we find expressions like "danced *before* the Lord" and "with all *their* might." But under the New Covenant we can worship *in the Spirit* and do things in the power of *His* might.

Again, in John 4:23 Jesus said:

> **But the hour cometh, and now is, when the**
> **true worshippers shall worship the Father *in spirit***
> ***and in truth*: for the Father seeketh such to**
> **worship him** (italics added for emphasis).

PUT ON THE OUTSIDE WHAT IS ON THE INSIDE

Only a New Testament worshipper can worship in Spirit and in truth.

Being a New Testament worshipper is not just doing something on the *outside*, but doing something on the *inside* also.

Now some people just want to do something on the inside. They say, "I just worship God in my own quiet way." But that isn't right either.

We need to put on the outside what is on the inside!

GETTING TO KNOW GOD

If we are going to be true New Testament worshippers, we

must have fellowship with God. Not just a relationship, but fellowship. Not just knowing *about* Him, but really *knowing Him*.

I traveled with a well-known minister for several years, and friends of mine would ask me questions such as, "What is he like?" or, "What is it like to know him?"

For the first couple of years that I traveled with him, I didn't know him. I knew about him by having read his books and heard his tapes. I heard him preach night after night until I could quote some of his stories word for word, but I didn't really know him. It wasn't until I had been with him a few years and we had spent time together that I got to know him. Then the better I got to know him, the easier it was for us to work together and flow with the Spirit in those meetings.

Once you get to know a person in a natural relationship, you can almost answer for him. When someone asks him a question, you will know exactly how he is going to answer.

You can get to know God that same way. Not just know *about* Him, but really *know Him*.

Now you may go to church and lift your hands to God, and it may look to other people like you are fellowshipping with Him, but it could be the same with you as it was with me and the minister I was traveling with. I knew all about him, but there was no *real* relationship until we had started spending time together and getting to know one another.

If you are going to be a true New Testament worshipper, you have to get to know God and learn to be led by the Spirit of God. You will find then that it isn't hard to spend time in God's presence. It's wonderful when you really get to know Him! You can learn how He speaks and what He likes, and you can begin to know about His character.

How do you get to know Him that way?

By learning His Word and by fellowshipping with Him. Not one or the other — both!

MINISTERING TO THE LORD

You can actually minister to the Lord. That may sound strange to some people. You might even say, "I thought the Lord was supposed to minister to us."

He does minister to us, but we can minister to Him also. Acts 13:2 says:

> **As they ministered to the Lord, and fasted, the Holy Ghost said....**

There are times when we should get apart from everything else and just minister to the Lord, especially if we need Him to speak to us in a certain area of our lives. According to this Scripture verse, that's the kind of atmosphere in which He speaks. Did you notice that? Again, it says, **As they ministered to the Lord, and fasted, the Holy Ghost said....** After they had ministered to Him, then He spoke to them!

As New Testament believers, we are privileged to have the Spirit of God dwelling on the inside of us. He is our Teacher, our Guide, our Helper, and He is living inside us!

It is easy for us to be led by our spirit if we take time to get to know Him. There are no formulas today like there were under the Old Covenant. We don't do things by ritual or form the way they did then. Again, in John 4:23,24 Jesus said:

> **But the hour cometh, and now is, when the true worshippers shall worship the Father *in spirit and in truth*: for the Father seeketh such to worship him.**
>
> ***God is a Spirit: and they that worship him must worship him in spirit and in truth*** (italics added for emphasis).

❀

OUT OF YOUR BELLY SHALL FLOW

CHAPTER 2

❀

OUT OF YOUR BELLY SHALL FLOW

COME AND DRINK

In the last day, that great day of the feast, Jesus stood and cried, saying, If any man thirst, let him *come* unto *me*, and drink (italics added for emphasis).

He that believeth on me, as the scripture hath said, out of his belly shall flow rivers of living water.

John 7:37,38

The Amplified Bible in verse 37 refers to this last day of the Feast as **the final and most important day**.

When you are speaking about something that is most important to you, you might refer to it as the "last" because you want people to catch it and then remember it.

Also, verse 37 in *The Amplified Bible* says, **Jesus stood, and He cried in a loud voice**. If He cried in a *loud* voice, there is, without a doubt, something here that He wants us to get hold of and understand!

DO YOU QUALIFY?

Before we go any further, you need to see if you qualify.

Jesus said in John 7:37, **If any man thirst....** Are you *man*? Of course you are. Even women are *man*! When the Bible refers to *man*, it is not talking about the male species; it's talking about the "man-kind," the "hu-man." We all qualify so far!

Again, He said in verse 37, **If any man thirst....** Now we may start losing some people here.

It isn't enough for you just to be a man — you have to thirst.

It isn't enough for you just to thirst — you have to come to Jesus.

But that isn't enough either!

It certainly seems that coming to Jesus should be enough, but there is something else you have to do. What is it? Drink!

Jesus continued in verse 37:

> **If any man thirst, let him come unto me, and drink.**

DO YOUR OWN DRINKING

I see people coming to Jesus all the time. Some of them drink; some don't. Some of them are just sitting there waiting for something to happen.

A friend of mine says there are three kinds of people in the world: those who make things happen, those who wait for things to happen and those who wonder what's happening!

Be someone who makes things happen.

Jesus has already done all He is ever going to do about your receiving from Him. He has given you His Word, but you have to act on it if you are going to see any results. If you want the Spirit of God to flow out of you — out of your belly, as the Bible says — you have to drink!

But you have to do your own drinking.

When you are thirsty, would you say to someone else, "I'm thirsty — would you take a drink for me?"

Of course not! You take a drink for yourself. You do your own drinking.

For you to get anything from God, you have to get it *His* way. God isn't like Burger King where you can have it *your* way. It's *His* way — or not at all! God doesn't bless *your* plans; He blesses *His* plans.

"SOCIAL DRINKERS"

A lot of Christians today are just "social drinkers," spiritually speaking, of course.

Do you know what "social drinkers" are? Those who come in and take just a little sip. Not enough to really affect them. They don't stay long, and they look the same going out as they did when they came in. They aren't affected at all.

When I was preaching this message in Europe, I found out that these spiritual social drinkers are called "occasional drinkers" over there. But it's the same thing.

Many people are that way in our churches. The pastor has to be careful when saying a prayer at the end of the service. He may look up and see half the people leaving, trying to beat one another out to the parking lot. Those people are "social drinkers."

But I want to be drunk on the Holy Ghost! I want to get all I can from Him. I want to be full of Him, not full of me.

How about you?

When you are full of yourself, the Spirit of God can't give you utterance in any area.

You might say, "But what will people think if I get wild?" Probably nothing. If you care what people think about you, you probably aren't going to do much for God anyway. We need to be pleasers of God, not pleasers of man.

ARE YOU FULL OF YOURSELF, OR FULL OF <u>HIM</u>?

When I was a kid, I worked in a bar, washing dishes in the back. Late at night on weekends when I heard the music start to play, I would run and look out the little round window on the door between the bar and the kitchen. I wanted to see all the people who were there. I had never seen a drunk person before.

I remember the first time I did that. It shocked me to see some of the prominent people in the community for whom I had respect and admiration. They had always seemed so self-controlled, so dignified. But I saw them out there dancing, with their hair getting so messed up and their clothes looking so sloppy.

Every weekend I watched them making fools of themselves, and I loved it. All through the week when I saw them out in the community, everything seemed so perfect. That's when they were "full of themselves." But when they came to the bar on weekends, they got full of something else.

DRUNK IN THE HOLY GHOST

In Ephesians, chapter 5, the apostle Paul wrote to the church at Ephesus, but this principle applies to the Church wherever we are. I want you to realize that the Bible is God speaking to you. Paul said:

> **And be not drunk with wine, wherein is excess; but be filled with the Spirit.**
>
> **Ephesians 5:18**

The Bible likens being full of the Holy Ghost to being full of wine. We could say also that it likens being *drunk* in the Holy Ghost to being *drunk* on wine!

We lose some people right away when we start talking about

being drunk in the Holy Ghost. But if you will just hold on for a minute, you will see what the Bible says about it. What if the Bible were to tell you it's God's will for you to be drunk in the Holy Ghost?

GOD'S WILL FOR YOU

We have read in Ephesians 5:18 about being filled with the Spirit. Now look at verse 17, with the italics added for emphasis:

> **Wherefore be ye not *unwise*, but understand-
> ing what the will of the Lord is.**

I don't know about you, but I want to be a wise person. And I imagine the most commonly asked question in the Body of Christ would be, What is God's will for me?

Then Scripture goes on in verse 18 and tells us what to do to be wise and what God's will is for our lives. It says, "Be not filled with wine, but be filled with the Spirit."

How do you do that?

The same way you get filled with wine: you drink!

This is what Jesus was talking about in John 7:37: **If any man thirst, let him come unto me, and drink.** You come to Him and drink.

BE BEING FILLED . . . CONTINUALLY

In Ephesians 5:18 it means in the Greek to be being filled.[1] It isn't just talking about a one-time experience. It's a continual process.

Some people will say, "I've already been filled with the Spirit." But it doesn't matter when you *first* got filled; it matters when you *last* got filled!

Paul was writing here to the Ephesians. They were filled

with the Holy Ghost in Acts, chapter 19, but he is telling them to be filled *again* and to keep on doing it — *continually!*

In Acts, chapter 2, we find the initial outpouring of the Spirit. But the same believers who were filled in Acts 2 were filled again in Acts 4! Acts 4:31 says, **they were all filled with the Holy Ghost**. If it were a "one-time thing," why would the same ones who were filled in chapter 2 have to be filled again in chapter 4? It isn't a one-time thing!

Be being filled...continually!

THE HOLY GHOST FELL . . . AGAIN!

A well-known minister said to me recently, "But being drunk in the Spirit only happened one time in the Bible — in Acts, chapter 2. You can't base anything on something that only happened once."

That's true; you can't base anything on something that just happened once. But I found another Scripture verse that verifies this teaching.

In Acts 11:15 Peter, telling about another experience, said:

> **And as I began to speak, the Holy Ghost fell on them,** *as on us at the beginning* (italics added for emphasis).

What happened when the Holy Ghost fell on believers at the beginning? Did they have healings and miracles right at that moment? No. They got drunk in the Holy Ghost!

They had healings and miracles later, but first they got filled with the Spirit of God. So much so, that they couldn't contain it anymore, and it started flowing "out of their bellies"! That's when they went rocking and reeling out into the streets of Jerusalem!

FULL FOR SERVICE

Before we go out into the world, we need to get full just like those believers did on the Day of Pentecost.

When you become full of the Holy Ghost, you receive a boldness that you don't get any other way.

We have seen this come on people sometimes in Holy Ghost meetings. The Spirit falls just like He did in the book of Acts, and people do things they normally would *never* do. It was against their character for the people to do what they did in Acts, chapter 2!

In John 20:19 the Bible says the disciples were hid away with the doors shut for fear of the Jews. But after they got full of the Holy Ghost, they went out preaching openly in the streets!

When you get full, you will probably act differently, too. But don't fight it; God is getting you full.

IT MAKES YOU <u>BOLD</u>!

Someone actually said to me, "The Holy Ghost doesn't fall today; He only fell on the Day of Pentecost."

I wondered if he ever read his Bible. I could understand if this was hidden over in the book of Lamentations, but it's right there in the book of Acts!

Every believer living in the last days ought to have a regular diet of the book of Acts! The Holy Ghost still falls today, just as He did in Acts 2:2, 4:31, 10:44, 11:15 and 16:26.

What happens when the Holy Ghost falls?

Buildings shake. People shake. And the devil shakes! People run and dance and shout!

What is happening to these believers?

Out of their bellies are flowing!

33

YIELDING TO THE HOLY GHOST

Don't think you would ever go out on the streets and lay hands on someone when the Holy Ghost is leading you if you won't even yield to Him when He is moving on you in a church service.

If people won't respond to God in praise during a church service when they are surrounded by people who love the moving of the Spirit, don't think they will respond to God out in the world when they are surrounded by people who are against the move of God.

THE KINGDOM OF GOD

It's time for the Church to forget about being popular with the world, trying to come up with programs that won't offend anyone in order to win people into the Kingdom.

The Bible says in Romans 14:17:

> **The kingdom of God is...righteousness, and peace, and joy in the Holy Ghost.**

We have always been big on the "righteousness" part and on the "peace" part. Now we are getting big on the "joy in the Holy Ghost" part!

The world is looking for joy. They spend untold fortunes just trying to get a little joy for a week or two. We need to let them know that there is a river that flows from the inside of us. What's in that river? Righteousness, peace and joy in the Holy Ghost!

Can anyone have it? Yes, anyone who is thirsty.

Are you thirsty? All you have to do is come to Jesus and drink. Thank God, it will last for more than a week or two! It *never* runs dry!

CHAPTER 3

❀

DANCING IN THE SPIRIT

❀

DANCING IN THE SPIRIT

YIELDING TO THE HOLY GHOST

The Holy Ghost will come on you and get in your feet if you will yield to Him. Now I'm not talking about the "Tulsa two-step" or the "Charismatic bunny hop." I'm talking about really dancing in the Holy Ghost!

You may ask, "What good does all that do?"

Among other things, it teaches you to know His voice and to learn to yield to the Spirit, which is vital for believers in these last days.

The Holy Ghost is not like the devil. The devil will try to *force* you to do something. The Holy Ghost will only prompt you. It is totally up to you whether you will yield to His prompting.

SPRING UP, O WELL

Sometimes after we dance in the Spirit, we might say, "I couldn't help it; something just came over me!"

That's true, something did come *on* us. It was the anointing of the Holy Ghost. And really we could help it if we tried hard enough, but who wants to?

There is nothing in your life that will give you more joy than yielding to the Holy Ghost!

Sometimes when that "well" starts springing up on the

inside of you, you feel like you are going to burst if you don't express it and let it out.

My wife and I do as much dancing in the Spirit at home as we do in church. We will be walking around the house praying about a situation when suddenly the anointing will fall, and we will start dancing. As I heard a minister say one time, "Nothing we preach is any good if it doesn't work at home."

IN THE FLESH

Some people are afraid that they will get "in the flesh" or that it will be "just them" doing it.

Well, it *will* be them doing it — it won't be their neighbor!

Besides that, most people are more "in the flesh" sitting back *not* yielding to God than they are by stepping out. Not yielding to the Holy Ghost *is* being in the flesh.

AN UNCTION FROM THE HOLY GHOST

Dancing in the Holy Ghost is not something you learn. You can't teach another person how to dance in the Holy Ghost any more than you can teach him or her how to speak in tongues. It is an unction that comes from the Spirit of God.

God gave us the *pattern* of praise and worship under the Old Covenant, but He gives us the *unction* under the New Covenant.

BALLET DANCING

I've actually been in churches that have held dance classes for their worship services. It is unscriptural to do that in a New Testament church. We have been in meetings, and right during the worship service dancers will come out in tights and get right up in front of the church and start ballet dancing. I can't imagine how anyone can think that draws attention to, or glorifies God.

You may have a program that has a choreographed dance in it — that's a performance. When you are worshipping God, you are not performing. When you dance in the spirit, it is mainly for your benefit. Others may be blessed, but you are not doing it to be seen of them; you are doing it to worship and praise God. It is a spontaneous outflow from your spirit, from the river on the inside. John 7:38 says, **Out of your belly shall flow....**! It's by the unction of the Holy Ghost.

DAVID DANCED BEFORE THE LORD

When David danced "before the Lord" in the Old Testament, it was a type of dancing "in the Spirit." Let's look at 2 Samuel 6:14:

> **And David danced before the Lord with all his might; and David was girded with a linen ephod.**

First of all, there are two key phrases here that we talked about earlier. First, in the Old Testament they danced "before the Lord" and New Testament believers dance "in the Spirit." Secondly, David danced "with all his might," and we do things in the power of "God's might."

A TYPE OF THE ANOINTING

Also, notice this verse says that David was wearing a linen ephod. That was a priestly garment, or a type of the anointing.

The reason David was dancing is because he saw the ark of the Covenant coming back to Jerusalem! The ark was where the presence of God dwelt. So really, this is a type of dancing in the Spirit, in the presence of the Lord. If David could dance like that under the shadow, what should we be doing in the Light?

If you have ever seen anyone dance in the Spirit, you can easily tell the difference between that and what we call just dancing "before" the Lord.

PENTECOSTAL PIONEER

A good friend of mine gave me an article written by Maria Woodworth-Etter, a Pentecostal pioneer. This article absolutely amazed me. I was surprised to see that what seems to us to be such a contemporary issue was the same point she was dealing with nearly one hundred years ago. This writing dates somewhere between 1892 and 1920.

Among the acts God is performing in these last days is dancing in the Spirit. These manifestations are not induced by suggestion or imitation. It is true that some will occasionally step and hop about, who are simply expressing their joy in their own way, as all of us in the former days have seen the saints, when they are blessed, run and skip and jump in holiness meetings. These manifestations cannot be regarded as sinful, and certainly are not hypocritical. They are the human expression of feeling toward God under great blessing, just as demonstrations at a baseball or football game are the natural, human expression of feeling in that lower, carnal place of joy. But the real dancing in the Spirit is altogether different. It is spontaneous. It comes without premeditation. It lacks all human direction and control. It does not follow the two-step or waltz or any dance ever learned. The steps are controlled and directed by the Holy Spirit. The whole body is energized by the Spirit. The movements are wonderfully graceful, and often rapid beyond all possibility of imitation. There are none of the attitudes or poses of familiar joining of partners, which characterize the ordinary dance.[1]

SQUARE DANCING

In Kenneth Hagin's book, *Plans, Purposes and Pursuits*, he talks about a meeting in Omaha, Nebraska, when the Spirit of God started to move, but then this couple got up in front and started to square-dance.

> The Spirit of God had started to move, but when they did that, the Spirit lifted. Then I came out and began to exhort on the difference between dancing in the flesh and dancing in the Spirit, and the Holy Ghost came on me and I started dancing in the Spirit, and it brought the anointing back in the room. I didn't plan on doing that, but the anointing came on me, and I yielded to Him. I personally think the reason people do things like the square dancers did is because they sense the moving of the Spirit and they don't know how to respond to it, so they revert to something that is familiar to them to express it instead of stepping out in faith. When the unction comes on you to dance, you step out, and the Holy Ghost will meet you.[2]

FOLLOW PEOPLE YOU CAN TRUST

We have to be taught the things of the Spirit and how to flow with the Spirit. That's why we need to listen to our fathers in the faith.

I want to follow those who have had great success in their ministries. Not someone who was hot for a little while. Not someone else who is hot for the moment. We must follow those who have had a proven track record through the years.

The Bible says in 2 Chronicles 20:20, **believe his prophets, so shall ye prosper**. Not someone who calls himself a prophet, but someone who *is* a prophet.

DANCING IN GOD'S HOUSE

In Luke 15, starting in verse 11, we see the parable of the lost son, who came home after wasting his inheritance in riotous living. This is a picture of a sinner coming back to God.

Verse 25 tells us what "God's house" is like. When the other brother came in from working in the field, **he heard musick and *dancing*** (italics added for emphasis). It didn't say he *saw* dancing; it says he *heard* dancing! There would have to be some pretty good dancing for it to be heard outside the house! There was dancing and music and rejoicing.

This was Jesus giving us a picture of what "God's house" is like. The Bible says:

> **Let them praise his name in the dance....**
>
> **Psalm 149:3**
>
> **Thou hast turned for me my mourning into dancing....**
>
> **Psalm 30:11**

Thank God, He has turned our mourning into dancing!

Thank God, the Church is getting full of joy. We aren't mourning anymore; we have entered into the joy and the presence of the Lord!

FALLEN GODS

I was singing in a Holy Ghost meeting one time with several other ministers at the convention center in Los Angeles, California. Right next door to us, a religious meeting was going on.

When I was on stage singing, I noticed one of the men from that meeting came in. I could tell immediately that he was mad. We quickly found out the reason for his anger.

Their religious group had altars built up in the front of the room. They had their gods sitting on those altars and they were worshipping them. When we had started praising God and dancing, the floor began to shake in our room. Then that caused the floor in their room to shake, and all their gods fell off their altars!

Thank God that our God is immovable! He is unshakable! The more we dance and praise Him, the more He likes it. Our God's house is full of music and dancing!

CHAPTER 4

❀

LIFTING UP YOUR VOICE

CHAPTER 4

❦

LIFTING UP YOUR VOICE

FOR YOURSELF

We talked earlier about Ephesians 5:17,18. Again, it says:

> **Wherefore be ye not unwise, but understanding what the will of the Lord is.**
>
> **And be not drunk with wine, wherein is excess; but be filled with the Spirit.**

Then Ephesians 5:19 goes on to say:

> **Speaking to yourselves in psalms and hymns and spiritual songs, singing and making melody in your heart to the Lord.**

By keeping this verse in context with the previous verses, you will see that it continues talking about drinking. Here is one way to take a drink.

Every believer should be doing this. It is not just for *singers* or *psalmists*; it is for the entire Body of Christ.

You should be speaking in psalms and singing songs in your own personal devotions to the Lord. Not songs you already know, but new ones that come up out of your spirit. These songs are just between you and God.

I attended a songwriters' seminar one time. The instructor told how people will come to him and say, "God gave me this song." Then after he hears it, he thinks God gave it to them because *He* didn't want it! Of course he was joking, but there may be some truth to that.

Sometimes when God ministers to us by giving us a word or a thought, it means so much to us that we want to share it with everyone. But some things are meant just for us.

Ephesians 5:19 begins with the words, **Speaking to yourselves**. You should be lifting up your voice to God all by yourself. As a matter of fact, most of the time these words are for your own benefit, not for the public (1 Corinthians 14:26).

FOR OTHERS

There is a companion Scripture to Ephesians 5:17-19. It is Colossians 3:16, which says:

> **Let the word of Christ dwell in you richly in all wisdom; teaching and admonishing one another in psalms and hymns and spiritual songs, singing with grace in your hearts to the Lord.**

This verse is talking not just about something you do by yourself, but about something you may do in a public assembly.

It starts out with this statement: **Let the word of Christ dwell in you richly**. You need to make sure that you are full of the Word of God before you ever get up in front of other people.

Then this verse continues by talking about sharing this word with others. Notice that whether a word is to yourself or to others, it is still to the Lord.

PSALMS, HYMNS, SPIRITUAL SONGS

You may be asking yourself, "What are psalms, hymns and spiritual songs?"

The definitions that I am about to share with you are the best I have ever found.

PSALM

Psalm: a spiritual poem or ode.

A psalm may be sung or it may be recited. Most of the time it will come out of your own personal prayer time. Often it will be the interpretation of a message you spoke in tongues. The best examples to be found are the book of Psalms in the Bible.

HYMN

Hymn: a song of praise and worship addressed to and directed toward God that will lift up, exalt and magnify God for Who He is.

It is important to note that some songs, which are called hymns, are not really hymns. Just because a song can be found in a church hymnal does not make it a hymn.

SPIRITUAL SONG

Spiritual song: a song that would bring forth the revelation of the Word that the Holy Ghost has given.

Many times in a church service someone will be given a spiritual song on the spur of the moment about the message that was just preached. Often, a spiritual song will illustrate the message. Also, you may receive a song in your own prayer time as you are meditating on certain Scriptures.

According to the last Scripture verse we read — Colossians 3:16 — psalms, hymns and spiritual songs should always do something. What should they do? They should teach us, admonish us and edify us. Anything that is inspired by the Spirit of God will *always* edify.

THE BEST WAY TO PRAISE GOD

Lifting up your voice is the most talked about form of praise in the New Testament. It's the best offering of praise you can give to God. Interestingly enough though, sometimes it can be hardest for believers to do this for any period of time.

If a worship leader tells a group of people to lift up their voices to God, usually within fifteen or twenty seconds they will stop to see what the leader will do next. It's easy for them to jump up and down and to clap all night long, but they can only lift their voices for a short time before they will want to move on.

I believe the devil has tried to keep members of the Body of Christ from lifting up their voices because he knows the power that it releases.

I have been in some meetings where people have "shouted the power down." They shouted unto God until His presence came in like a wind, then people all around the building began falling under that power.

MAGNIFY GOD

We need to magnify God with our voices.

What does it mean to magnify God?

It would be like taking a magnifying glass and holding it over the words on a page. The words aren't really any bigger than they were before; they just look bigger.

God is already big, but it doesn't do you any good unless He looks big to you!

How does God get bigger to you?

By your magnifying Him. By the lifting of your voice to Him in worship and praise.

A REAL SACRIFICE OF PRAISE

Hebrews 13:15 says:

> **By him therefore let us offer the sacrifice of praise to God continually, that is, *the fruit of our lips* giving thanks to his name** (italics added for emphasis).

What does it mean to offer up a sacrifice of praise to God?

We have usually interpreted it to mean we are to praise Him when we don't *feel* like it.

Well, that's true; we should praise Him when we *feel* like it and when we *don't* feel like it. But that isn't what this Scripture verse is talking about.

When I had finished studying the first five books of the Old Testament, I was able to understand about *sacrifices* in a way that I had never understood before. In the Old Testament, when God's people brought a sacrifice to Him, it was the *best* that they had. They wouldn't even consider coming to God without a sacrifice and without it being the best they had to offer.

The Scripture we looked at in Hebrews 13 was written, of course, to *Hebrew* Christians. They understood some particulars about sacrifices that we may not have realized.

This verse is literally telling us how to enter into the presence of God with the best sacrifice we can bring Him. For New Testament believers, the Bible tells us the best sacrifice we can bring to God is the lifting up of our voices!

> *...the fruit of our lips* **giving thanks to his name** (italics added for emphasis).
>
> **Hebrews 13:15**

JONAH

When Jonah was in the belly of a great fish, his deliverance came after he lifted his voice to God in thanksgiving as a sacrifice.

> **When my soul fainted within me I remem-
> bered the Lord: and my prayer came in unto thee,
> into thine holy temple.**
>
> **They that observe lying vanities forsake their
> own mercy.**
>
> **But *I will sacrifice unto thee with the voice of
> thanksgiving* [italics added for emphasis]; I will pay
> that that I have vowed. Salvation is of the Lord.**
>
> **And the Lord spake unto the fish, and it
> vomited out Jonah upon the dry land.**
>
> **Jonah 2:7-10**

Jonah's answer came after he sacrificed unto God with a
voice of thanksgiving!

PAUL AND SILAS

That's what Paul and Silas were doing in Acts, chapter 16.
They were lifting their voices in praise to God. Look at verses 25
and 26:

> **And at midnight Paul and Silas prayed, and
> sang praises unto God: and the prisoners heard
> them.**
>
> **And suddenly there was a great earthquake,
> so that the foundations of the prison were shaken:
> and immediately all the doors were opened, and
> every one's bands were loosed.**

When you begin to praise God, it affects not only you but
those around you! Not only were Paul and Silas's bands loosed,
everyone's bands were loosed!

Did you notice *when* the answer came to Paul and Silas?
While they were praising God! That's often when *your* answer
will come, too.

HEALED WHILE PRAISING

I remember hearing a story that Dr. Lilian B. Yeomans told about a missionary to China. This missionary had contracted a severe case of smallpox, so she had been quarantined to her room and was expected to die.

While all alone there in her room, she had a vision. She saw one of those old-fashioned scales, the kind with two baskets balancing each other. One basket was full and weighted down with her *prayers*. The other basket held her *praises* — but it was almost empty!

The Lord told her in the vision that when the *praise* side balanced out the *prayer* side, her answer would come. So she began to lift her voice in praise to God. She began to shout and sing unto God! It took her a few days to fill up that *praise* side because she had been *praying* the whole time and had done very little *praising*.

The people outside the room probably thought she was going crazy or was delirious. But after a few days she walked out of the room where she had been sent to die. She was fully healed, fully recovered, fully restored! Her answer came while she was praising God!

Notice Philippians 4:6, with italics added for emphasis:

Be careful for nothing; but in every thing by prayer and supplication *with thanksgiving* let your requests be made known unto God.

How do we do that? By lifting our voice to God and thanking Him after we pray. We are thanking Him in advance for the answer. That's what faith will do. We don't shout when the walls fall; we shout the walls down!

ENCOURAGE YOURSELF IN THE LORD

Some people have said to me, "I would lift my voice to God more than I do, but I run out of things to say."

I understand what they mean.

But really, if you did what David did in 1 Samuel 30:6, you would never run out of things to say. This Scripture says he **encouraged himself in the Lord his God**. *The Amplified Bible* says, **David encouraged and strengthened himself in the Lord his God.**

What does it mean to "encourage yourself in the Lord"? It means to remind God of what He has already done for you.

David reminded God of the lion and the bear. He reminded God of the victory over Goliath.

So you have to remind God of the victories He has brought you through and then thank Him for it. Thank Him for what He is doing right now in your life. Thank Him for what lies ahead in your future. Thank Him in advance for what He is getting ready to do in you and through you. That will strengthen you.

SHOUT!

If you need some walls to come down in any area of your life, shout them down! Faith shouts before the walls come down.

You start putting this into practice, and you will see the changes it will make in your life.

TEHILLAH: TO SING PRAISES

We lift our voices to God by speaking, by shouting and by singing. With the italics added for emphasis, Psalm 100, verse 4, says:

> Enter into his gates with thanksgiving, and
> into his courts with *praise*: be thankful unto him,
> and bless his name.

The Hebrew word translated "praise" is *tehillah*, which means "glory; praise; song of praise; praiseworthy deeds."[1] We enter into the presence of God by singing praises.

In 1 Corinthians 14:15 Paul said, **I will sing with the spirit, and I will sing with the understanding also.**

Hebrews 2:12 says, **I will declare thy name unto my brethren, in the midst of the church will I sing praise unto thee.**

James 5:13 says, **Is any among you...merry? let him sing psalms.**

CREATING AN ATMOSPHERE

Lifting up our voices in song is something we all should be doing. Music is very important in the Church today. It often creates an atmosphere for God to move. Music can "set the stage," so to speak. God knew this before Hollywood did.

Have you ever been watching a movie or a television show and been able to tell by the music when something was about to happen? The music was preparing you.

Our praise and worship today should do the same thing. It should prepare us and take us into the place where God wants us and where we should want to be: in His presence.

THE GLORY OF THE LORD

> Also the Levites which were the singers, all
> of them of Asaph, of Heman, of Jeduthun, with
> their sons and their brethren, being arrayed in
> white linen, having cymbals and psalteries and

harps, stood at the east end of the altar, and with them an hundred and twenty priests sounding with trumpets:

It came even to pass, as the trumpeters and singers were as one, to make one sound to be heard in praising and thanking the Lord; and *when they lifted up their voice* with the trumpets and cymbals and instruments of musick, and praised the Lord, saying, For he is good; for his mercy endureth for ever: that then the *house was filled with a cloud*, even the house of the Lord;

So that the priests could not stand to minister by reason of the cloud: for the *glory of the Lord had filled the house of God* (italics added for emphasis).

2 Chronicles 5:12-14

The singers were **arrayed in white linen** as they began to sing. That is a type of the anointing.

We talked in chapter 3 about "garments" in the Old Testament often referring to the anointing. In the Old Testament it was important what they had on the *outside*. Under the New Testament it is important what we have on the *inside*.

When God's people began to sing or play an instrument with a type of the anointing to the Lord, the glory of God filled the house.

AN UNSEEN FORCE

I have been in meetings where the glory of God filled the house. One time I was with Kenneth Hagin, ministering at a meeting in Lakeland, Florida, and the glory of God came into the room.

When we tried to get up the steps onto the platform to assist him, we couldn't make it. It was like running into an unseen force. The anointing was so strong that we had to hold on to the rail of the steps to keep from falling over.

We tried a second time to go up the steps, but it happened again. We had to stand there for a long time leaning over the rail before we could even move.

God is wanting to fill the Church with His glory!

WHILE WE WERE SINGING

I was at another meeting singing when the glory of God came in the room. The minister told us to continue singing because the anointing was on us. There were five people over in the wheelchair section, and while we were singing, three of them got up and started walking! No one touched them — they just responded to the glory of God!

I have been in several meetings, with different ministers as well as out on my own, when God's glory came in the room. As we were singing and praising God, people were miraculously healed, changed and delivered! We have heard testimonies of tumors disappearing and deaf ears being opened while we were singing and worshipping the Lord during our meetings.

BECAUSE HE WAS THERE

There is just something about creating an atmosphere for God to move.

The testimonies I just shared with you didn't happen because *we* were there. On many occasions we didn't even know what happened in the meeting until people contacted us later and told us. It wasn't because *we* were there; it was because *He* was there!

God knows exactly what you need and how to get it to you.

He inhabits, or dwells in, the praises of His people. And when He shows up, things happen!

SEEING THE GLORY

I remember a particular meeting in New Braunfels, Texas, when we had been singing and shouting. I ran around the room, and people were dancing in the Spirit all over the place! We had been singing to God for about an hour when everyone spontaneously began lifting their voices in praise and worship to God.

After a few minutes, I opened my eyes. It was like a fog had entered throughout the room. For years I had heard people talking about seeing God's glory, but I had never seen it for myself. I had sensed it, but this was the first time I had ever seen it. It was interesting to me, because the atmosphere was charged with what seemed like electricity.

We can sometimes put God in a box, thinking we always have to be quiet and in the kind of atmosphere that we would call "worshipful" in order for God's presence to come in like He did then. But we weren't being so quiet. We were raising our voices, praising and worshipping our God. Then He showed up and put His approval on that offering. At least thirty people received their healing in that moment of the manifested presence of God.

Another minister began operating in the gifts of the Spirit, and people responded all over the auditorium. God's glory came in that room when we were singing, running, dancing and shouting!

Lifting your voice to God is not just *one* way that you can praise Him; it's the *best* way.

The "fruit of our lips" *is* the sacrifice the Bible tells us in Hebrews 13:15 to bring to God when we come into His presence. This is without question the most talked about form of praise or worship in the New Testament, or the Old for that matter. We should be lifting our voices in worship and praise to God more than anything else.

CHAPTER 5

❀

PRAISING GOD WITH OUR HANDS

CHAPTER 5

❀

PRAISING GOD WITH OUR HANDS

LIFTING OUR HANDS

It is amazing to me that one of the most controversial subjects on praise and worship today is what we do with our hands.

In both the Old and New Testaments, the Bible tells us exactly what to do with our hands in praise and worship to God. As was stated earlier in this study, we have to interpret the Old in light of the New.

So, what does the New Testament say we are to do with our hands?

First Timothy 2:8, with italics added for emphasis, says:

> I will therefore that men pray every where, *lifting up* holy hands, without wrath and doubting.

There are Old Testament Scriptures that coincide with this verse from 1 Timothy, chapter 2.

Psalm 63:4 says:

> Thus will I bless thee while I live: I will lift up my hands in thy name.

Psalm 134:2 says:

> Lift up your hands in the sanctuary, and bless the Lord.

In addition to the references which say we are to lift up our hands, there are over fifty references to the word *praise* that mean to lift our hands to God.[1] That's too many to mention in this space. It would take up the whole chapter!

HEBREW WORDS FOR "PRAISE"

Every time you see the word *praise* in some form in the Old Testament, it could have one of seven different meanings, such as lifting your hands, bowing down, lifting your voice and singing.

All of this is a praise to God, but there are many different methods of doing so. It is interesting to note that *not one* of the over 300 references to "praise" means to clap.

GREEK WORDS FOR "PRAISE"

In the New Testament the word *praise* is in the general sense of what we know it to mean. There is, however, one exception.

The word translated "praise" in 1 Corinthians 11:2, 17 and 22 is the Greek word *epaineo*, which means "to applaud."[2] The most important point to realize in this context is that this word is referring to *man*, not to *God*. It is saying, "I commend you" or "I applaud you." But this thought is being spoken from one man to another man.

CLAPPING OR APPLAUDING

So, what about clapping?

Jesus appeared to Kenneth Hagin in a vision in 1987 and told him that clapping is neither praise nor worship. When he first shared about the vision in Tulsa, Oklahoma, at Camp-meeting, some people didn't like it.

I paid especially close attention, because when I traveled with him, I would say at the close of his services, "Let's give the Lord a hand." It shocked me when he first said it, but then I saw that it lined up exactly with what the Word of God says.

There is only one isolated Scripture in the Bible about clapping your hands that even refers to God.

Psalm 47:1 says:

> **O clap your hands, all ye people; shout unto God with the voice of triumph.**

Notice it doesn't say clap your hands *to* God. It says clap your hands, but then it says *shout* unto God!

There are some Old Testament Scriptures that refer to clapping but only figuratively. For instance, Isaiah 55:12 says, **all the trees of the field shall clap their hands,** and Psalm 98:8 says, **Let the floods clap their hands.**

In the New Testament, the word *clap* isn't used at all!

When you are trying to see whether some action is scriptural, here is a good key to follow: look in the *Strong's Exhaustive Concordance*; if you can't find Scripture to back it up, then you can forget about it.

ARE WE SUPPOSED TO CLAP?

When I was holding a meeting with a gospel music group in California, one of its members was speaking during the meeting and said, "A prophet in Tulsa said we are not supposed to clap anymore." I could tell by the way he said it that he disagreed. He went on then to give his reasons for disagreeing, none of which lined up with the Word of God.

I knew exactly which meeting he was referring to. It was the same meeting I mentioned earlier in this chapter: Kenneth Hagin's meeting in Tulsa, Oklahoma. Let me point out a couple of things that are relevant.

First of all, I was at that meeting in Tulsa, and I knew *he* wasn't.

Second of all, when I was there, I heard it firsthand. *The minister never once said that we weren't supposed to clap anymore.* He said Jesus had appeared to him and told him that clapping wasn't praise or worship. As I discovered, the Bible backs up that idea one hundred percent.

No one said we weren't supposed to clap. We just aren't to do it at the wrong times, and we don't call it something that the Bible doesn't call it.

When Kenneth Hagin went on to share that vision, he said we were not to mix brass with gold. In other words, don't mix *pure* worship with a *substitute*. When Jesus appeared to him, He told him we have brought the clapping and dancing of the world into our church services, and that was mixing what is pure with what is not. When he shared that, I could see exactly what he was talking about.

So, what was Kenneth Hagin talking about?

SUBSTITUTING BRASS FOR GOLD

In 1 Kings, chapters 6 and 7, we see that everything in the temple was made of gold. But in 2 Chronicles 12:9,10 the gold was taken out of the temple and replaced with brass. It might look the same on the outside but would not be the same on the inside.

Brass isn't a pure metal, but a mixture. It is interesting that when they had the real thing, they didn't protect it or guard over it at all; but when they replaced it with the cheap substitute, they started guarding it! Second Chronicles 12, verse 10, says they committed the brass to the hands of the chief guard.

In many cases, people are still the same: they let go of the pure but want to hold on to the fake. Jesus Himself couldn't talk people out of it in many cases. There are people today who will hold on to something and fight for it, even when it has been proven through the Word that it is unscriptural. I have seen it firsthand.

A TIME TO CLAP

Now I am certainly not against clapping. I think there is a time to clap. Clapping to music would enhance it as much as playing percussion instruments. I am only pointing out what the Bible says about it in relation to praise or worship.

Clapping when you have a victory seems like a natural response, but that doesn't make it praise or worship if the Bible doesn't say it is.

DON'T BRING JESUS DOWN TO MAN'S LEVEL

People clap for one another. We clap when we hear a great speaker. So when we clap to Jesus, we are bringing Him down to man's level.

But Jesus is worthy of all honor and praise. He shouldn't be treated just like we would treat another human being.

We should do what the Bible tells us to do with our hands. As we read earlier in Psalm 134:2:

Lift up your hands...and bless the Lord.

BE LIKE A CHILD

What is a natural response when a little child comes to its father? Does it come up to him and clap in his face? Of course not; that would be obnoxious. The child comes to its father with uplifted hands.

It also would be obnoxious to God if we were to come into His throne room and start clapping in His face.

How then should we come to our God?

Just as a little child comes to its father here on earth: with uplifted hands.

CHAPTER 6

❀

SPIRITUAL WARFARE

CHAPTER 6

❧

SPIRITUAL WARFARE

AN OCCUPYING ARMY

For you to keep your doctrine straight on the subject of spiritual warfare, the most important point to realize is this: we are not a *conquering* army; we are an *occupying* army. Hallelujah! That should be good news to all of us.

Jesus was the *Conqueror*, and the Bible tells us in Romans 8:37 that He made us *more* than conquerors! We didn't do any of the work, but we still get all the benefits!

You need to remember this. There are a lot of different things happening in praise and worship music today where spiritual warfare is concerned.

THE GOOD FIGHT

The only fight we fight is the fight of faith, and as 1 Timothy 6:12 tells us, it is a *good* fight!

Once you get a revelation of 1 John 4:4, which says, **greater is he that is in you, than he that is in the world,** you won't even want to fight the devil.

Satan is *already* defeated! We need to take our eyes off of him and put them on God.

PULLING DOWN STRONGHOLDS

We hear a lot of things today about bombarding the gates of hell and pulling down strongholds over cities. It's like I heard a minister say once: "If you could pull down strongholds over a city, don't you think Paul would have done it over Ephesus or Jesus would have done it over Jerusalem?"

The scripture in Second Corinthians, chapter 10, about pulling down strongholds is talking about our thoughts and imaginations. That is where our battles are fought — in the mind.

We are going to affect cities the same way Jesus did and Paul did. They are the best two examples we have of men ministering under the anointing. Paul preached the Word the same way Jesus did. He went about the cities and villages teaching, preaching and healing.

We won't come up with some new revelation that Jesus or Paul didn't know. As a matter of fact, Jesus never dealt with demons except through His ministry to individuals.

STAND, STAND, STAND!

If you look in Ephesians 6, you will see that the armor is not to be used for attack, but to *withstand* the attacks of the devil! This armor is not offensive, but defensive. In just a few short verses, it says we are to *withstand*, *stand*, *stand* and *stand*! I don't think it can be made any plainer than that. It is obvious that Paul is trying to get something over to us.

When Jesus faced the devil, He *stood* His ground and spoke the Word (Luke 4:1-13). The Word is our weapon. Jesus didn't try to use any strange or unscriptural methods of warfare.

I have seen meetings advertised where people have had "pulling down strongholds over the city" meetings. I know some of the people who were involved in those meetings. Some of them are my friends. But I have been to those same cities since then, and they are no different. Situations in some of them might even be a little worse.

KNOW WHAT KINGDOM YOU ARE IN

You have to realize what kingdom you are in.

According to 2 Corinthians 4:4, Satan is the god of this world. He will hold that position until his lease runs out — and there is nothing we can do about it.

But if you are in the kingdom of God, then the kingdom of God is in you! As was pointed out earlier in this chapter, 1 John 4:4 says, **greater is he that is in you, than he that is in the world.**

TAKING CITIES

As believers, we operate by a different set of rules than does the world. We are not subject to its rules.

I am certainly not against taking cities for Jesus! But people are saved and cities are changed today the same way they were in the Bible: by preaching the Word and by the move of the Spirit.

Peter won *three thousand* souls in his first altar call on the Day of Pentecost, and *five thousand* after his second! How did he do it? They had a move of God — a sign and wonder. Then he preached! The sign pointed them toward God, and the preaching led them to God. Acts 2:47 tells us that the Lord added to the church daily. The disciples preached the Word and yielded to the Holy Ghost, then God brought in the people.

GOD'S PLAN FOR WARFARE

One of the best examples in the Bible on spiritual warfare

is found in 2 Chronicles, chapter 20. Verse 17, with italics added for emphasis, says:

> **Ye shall not need to fight in this battle: set yourselves, *stand ye still*.**

Now this is what they did in a natural battle, and this is what we do today in spiritual battles. This is the same as it says in Ephesians 6.

It goes on in 2 Chronicles 20:21:

> **And when he had consulted with the people, he appointed *singers* unto the Lord, and that should *praise* the beauty of holiness, as they went out before the army, and to *say*, Praise the Lord; for his mercy endureth for ever** (italics added for emphasis).

It's a good thing Jehoshaphat didn't ask some of us today what we should sing. We might tell him, "Let's sing about bombarding the gates of hell!" Thank God, Jesus said the gates of hell shall not prevail against the Church (Matthew 16:18).

God told those singers to sing these words: **Praise the Lord; for his mercy endureth for ever.** That was God's idea of what spiritual warfare is!

This is not something directed toward the devil. It is praise directed toward God! We are to be praising the beauty of holiness by *lifting up our voice* to God. That is spiritual warfare.

DON'T TRY TO REASON IT OUT

That's what Paul and Silas did in prison (see Acts 16). That's what the missionary from China did in the story we related in chapter 4 of this book. And that is what we should be doing today!

It doesn't sound much like warfare if you are thinking with your natural mind. If Jehoshaphat had tried to reason it out in his natural mind, he might have gotten into trouble himself.

TYPES OF THE ANOINTING

Second Chronicles 20:21 from *The Amplified Bible*, with italics added for emphasis, says Jehoshaphat:

> ...appointed singers to sing to the Lord and praise Him in their *holy [priestly] garments* as they went out before the army....

As we saw earlier, their *garments* in the Old Testament were a type of the anointing. So this is a type of singing under the anointing.

Can just singing to God under the anointing be spiritual warfare? The Bible proves that praising God is the best way for us to fight.

When you lift up God and exalt Him, that puts Him in authority over your situation. And if God be for you, who can be against you? (Romans 8:31)

PRAISE CONFUSES THE DEVIL

Continuing in 2 Chronicles, chapter 20, it says in verse 22:

> And when they began to sing and to praise, the Lord set ambushments against the children of Ammon, Moab, and mount Seir, which were come against Judah; and they were smitten.

It goes on to tell how they turned on each other. God confused them, and they killed one another!

Praise confuses the devil. Notice that their answer came while they were lifting their voices to God in praise.

JERICHO

Joshua fought the battle of Jericho and the walls came tumbling down! How did he do it? By following the directions *exactly* as the Lord had given them to him.

It certainly must have looked interesting to him. The city had walls so thick that chariot races could have been run on top of them, with chariots lined up seven abreast! The Lord's method to destroy the enemy was for God's people to march around the city six days without any word proceeding from their mouths. On the seventh time day, they would march around the city seven times, and on the seventh time, they would *shout*!

So it says in Joshua 6:16:

> **And it came to pass at the seventh time, when the priests blew with the trumpets, Joshua said unto the people, Shout; for the Lord hath given you the city.**

According to Joshua 6:2, the Lord had already given them the city. As far as God was concerned, it was already theirs.

What was their method of warfare?

Lifting their voices in a shout! And it works the same today.

OTHER SCRIPTURES

Psalm 149:6 says, **Let the high praises of God be in their mouth, and a two-edged sword in their hand.**

Ephesians 6:10 says, **be strong in the Lord, and in the power of *his* might** (italics added for emphasis). This Scripture never mentions that we are to be strong in our own might.

Psalm 24:8 says, **Who is the King of glory? The Lord**

strong and mighty, the Lord mighty in battle. It is the Lord Who is strong in battle, not us. We are to rely on *His* strength.

Second Chronicles 20:15 says, **Thus saith the Lord unto you, Be not afraid nor dismayed by reason of this great multitude; for the battle is not yours, but God's.**

FOR OUR ADMONITION

These Old Testament accounts of Joshua and Jehoshaphat are not just stories from which we learn history. In 1 Corinthians 10:6 it says these things happened to them for examples, or types, that were written for our admonition. It makes it easier to face battles in this life if we already know what to do to have the victory and we know that the Greater One abides, dwells and lives on the inside of us.

Just like everything else in our lives, our praise and worship music should line up with the Word of God. I'm eager to learn all I can about God's way of doing things. We should have songs about standing our ground, about who we are in Christ, about our authority as a believer. But according to the Word of God, the best method of spiritual warfare is for us to lift our voices to Him, to praise the beauty of holiness and to say, "Praise the Lord, for His mercy endureth forever!"

CHAPTER 7

❀

THE CORPORATE ANOINTING

CHAPTER 7

❦

THE CORPORATE ANOINTING

WE ARE THE TEMPLE OF THE HOLY GHOST

In the Old Testament the presence of God was kept shut
up in the Holy of Holies in Solomon's temple in Jerusalem.
But when Jesus died on the cross, the Bible tells us:

>**...the veil of the temple was rent in twain from
the top to the bottom....**
>
>**Matthew 27:51**

From that point on, God no longer would dwell in temples
made with hands. After the death, burial and resurrection of
Jesus, the Epistles were written to tell us that now *we* are the
house of God.

>**...for ye are the temple of the living God; as
God hath said, I will dwell in them, and walk in
them; and I will be their God, and they shall be
my people.**
>
>**2 Corinthians 6:16**
>
>**But Christ as a son over his own house; whose
house are we.**
>
>**Hebrews 3:6**

We as believers in Jesus Christ are now the temple of the
Holy Ghost! Our bodies are where the Spirit of God dwells.

The Bible tells us in Romans 12:1 to present our bodies a
living sacrifice to God. In the *King James Version* this verse ends
with these words, **which is your reasonable service,** while
The Amplified Bible adds the phrase, **and spiritual worship.**

Worship is not just something you do with your *hands* or your *voice*, but something you do with your *life*. True worship toward God is not just merely an action; it is an attitude you are to walk in consistently.

SOMETHING ON THE INSIDE

If you are filled on the inside with God, He will show up on the outside. Something on the inside working on the outside!

Romans, chapter 12, verse 2, in the Wuest translation says the following, with italics that are added for emphasis:

> **And stop assuming an outward expression that does not come from within you and is not representative of what you are in your inner being but is patterned after this age; but change your *outward expression* to one that comes from *within* and is representative of your inner being, by the renewing of your mind....**

THE TEMPLE OF GOD, COLLECTIVELY

First Corinthians 3:16 in *The Amplified Bible* says:

> **Do you not discern and understand that you [the *whole* church at Corinth] are God's temple (His sanctuary), and that God's Spirit has His permanent dwelling in you [to be at home in you, *collectively* as a church and also individually]?** (The italics were added for emphasis.)

Not only are we the temple of God *individually*, but the Body of Christ is the temple of God *collectively*. There is an anointing that comes on an *individual* to minister, but there is also an anointing that can come on an *entire group of believers* assembled together. This is called a "corporate anointing."

THE GLORY OF THE LORD

When we become as one, with one voice and one purpose, we will see what God's people saw in 2 Chronicles 5:13,14. With italics added for emphasis, these verses read:

> **It came even to pass, as the trumpeters and singers were as *one*, to make *one* sound to be heard in praising and thanking the Lord; and when they lifted up their voice with the trumpets and cymbals and instruments of musick, and praised the Lord, saying, For he is good; for his mercy endureth for ever: that then *the house was filled with a cloud*, even the house of the Lord;**

> **So that the priests could not stand to minister by reason of the cloud: *for the glory of the Lord* had filled the house of God.**

Thank God for the individual anointing, but there is nothing like the power of God that is made available by the corporate anointing when believers come together as one.

What we just read in 2 Chronicles is also for us today. We are under a new and better Covenant (Hebrews 8:6-10). If it happened under the Old Covenant, and the New is better, then it is for us today!

IN ONE ACCORD

Speaking of New Testament believers, Acts 1:14 says they **all continued with *one accord* in prayer and supplication.** Acts 2:1 says, **they were all with *one accord* in *one place*.** Acts 4:24 says, **they lifted up their voice to God with *one* accord.** (The italics were added for emphasis.)

For the sake of space, I won't tell you the results of these Scripture verses now. You need to look them up for yourself.

When you do that, notice the power of God that is made available by the corporate anointing.

THE BEST IS YET TO COME

Many believers have been in meetings where they have seen a display of a strong corporate anointing, but the best is yet to come!

The stories I have shared in this book relate some of my own experiences, but I am not satisfied with what I have seen so far. It's just a taste of what is to come!

You may have heard stories about meetings where the angels joined in and began singing with the congregation. You might even have heard it yourself or heard actual cassette tapes of such meetings.

I shared earlier about meetings I have attended where the glory of God came into the room like a cloud and people were healed all over the building. I saw people get up out of wheel-chairs while those in the congregation were lifting their voices to make one sound in praise to God.

But as wonderful as all these experiences have been, I believe that we have only seen limited results thus far. I know there has to be more.

How are we going to move into all God has for us? When will we start seeing the *best that is yet to come*?

HIS PLAN, HIS BLESSING

When we lay aside our *own* plans and our *own* ways of doing things, then we will start pursuing *God's* way of doing things. God doesn't bless *our* plans; He blesses *His* plan. He has already told us what to do to obtain that which He made available for the Body of Christ.

As far as praise and worship are concerned, there is little left to interpretation. The Bible tells us *exactly* what it is and how to create an atmosphere for God to move in. That should be our goal.

When we enter into the fullness of what God has already established in His Word, then we will see His blessing and His anointing come on us individually and corporately like we have never seen before.

Truly, *the best is yet to come!*

CHAPTER 8

❀

A "SIXTH" OFFICE OF MINISTRY?

❧

A "SIXTH" OFFICE OF MINISTRY?

PRAISE AND WORSHIP LEADERS

Leading praise and worship in a church service or some other gathering of believers is an interesting position to be in. That person is usually the only other person on the platform in a leadership position who is not in the fivefold ministry.

According to Ephesians 5:19 and Colossians 3:16, the leading of praise and worship would fall under the ministry of helps. As important as we know the music ministry is today, the New Testament says nothing about it, so it too would fall under the ministry of helps.

I have seen people try to make the leading of praise and worship the "sixth" office of ministry, but it is not. Instead, it is a helps ministry for the fivefold ministry. A person's goal as worship leader should be, "How can I help the pastor or the minister?"

LEADING, BUT NOT BEING THE LEADER

I have seen many worship leaders go on to become a part of the fivefold ministry. But as long as they are standing in the position of helps, that is their calling.

Leading worship is perhaps one of the most difficult positions any person could be in. He (or she) is leading but is not the leader. He is responsible to take people into a certain place spiritually, but often he has to do it the way someone else tells him. Then once he gets the service to where he feels it should be, he hands it over to someone else to flow in the ministry gift.

The worship leader should be just as prepared as the minister in charge of the service. He never knows where the Spirit of God might lead him in a service, and he has to be ready to handle whatever may come his way.

INSPIRING THE GIFT

In the Old Testament the prophet called on a minstrel for inspiration. Today the music ministry can be used to inspire all five offices of ministry.

The *only* office in the Old Testament was the prophet's ministry. Today living under the New Covenant, we have apostles, prophets, evangelists, pastors and teachers (Ephesians 4:11). The music ministry must be able to set the stage for all five of these gifts to operate.

TWO JOBS IN ONE

The worship leader must be in a position to lead others in praise and worship and, at the same time, inspire the ministry gift. That is not always an easy task. Sometimes it requires two different abilities.

One of the most challenging situations is when the worship leader feels led to do it one way, while the minister in charge wants it another way. What is the worship leader to do? He must always do whatever that minister wants.

The minister is the person in authority, the one responsible for the service. The worship leader should always be subjected to him (or her).

Many times the praise and worship leader is sure that God wanted to do something more in the service, but feels it got "cut off" before it reached the place it needed to be. Whenever a person is working with those who are in a higher position of authority, he must always submit his will to theirs. That is the scriptural thing to do.

PSALMISTS AND MINSTRELS

There are psalmists today and there are minstrels today, though we don't often use such terminology. In contemporary language, we refer to them as songwriters, singers and musicians. But that doesn't do away with the validity of their ministry.

It is important, however, to note that all songwriters are not psalmists and all musicians are obviously not minstrels.

Also, there are some fivefold ministers who stand in positions of music as well as in their main fivefold ministry gift. Any person who stands in the fivefold ministry should always put that calling first.

Although the psalmist's ministry is not one of the fivefold ministry gifts, that certainly doesn't make it any less important. It is the high calling of God on many people's lives.

CONSIDER THE ANOINTING FACTOR

Many people want to be a worship leader because they are singers; and since they got saved, it would seem the obvious move to make.

The question is, What are they *anointed* to do?

Are we talking about ability or talent? That generally is part of the equipment, but I have heard many people minister in music who were more anointed than the person who was more perfected in his skill as a musician. (When using the term *musician*, I am referring to any person who makes music; it could be a vocalist or an instrumentalist.)

So, how can you tell if someone is anointed? What is the measuring stick to use that will determine if the anointing is present? Will there be goose bumps running up and down your spine? As one minister said to me, "That was so anointed, it made the hair stand up on my arm."

That certainly may happen. But the way to tell if something or someone is anointed is by asking this question: Did it remove any burdens or destroy any yokes? According to Isaiah 10:27, that is what the anointing is for and that is what will happen when the anointing is present.

FLOWING WITH DIFFERENT MINISTERS

There is much that is left to interpretation when it comes to flowing with different ministers.

If you are a worship leader in a local church, you will generally be working with the same ministers. But if you work in meetings with various ministers as I do, it could be a bit different. Everyone is different.

There are some ministers I have worked with who know *exactly* what they want and how they want it. Most of the time, that makes my job easier. They will usually tell me what to do, and I just do exactly what they say.

On the other hand, there are ministers who aren't sure what they want, but they know when it *isn't* what they want. That creates a little more of a challenge for the worship leader. He has to find out what the ministers are looking for. Many times this can happen in the middle of the service right in front of a crowd.

Then there are ministers who just leave it up to the worship leader to flow the way God is leading him.

DIFFERENT STROKES

Some ministers think there is only one way to do things because that's how God uses them. I am in the position where I cross the borders of many different "camps" and see people anointed to minister in various ways. Often, people think, "This is the way God does things, and this is what is anointed." And for them, it is. They are exactly right.

For the next minister, that may not be the case. If he has one way of doing things, that is great, and that's probably how God uses him.

But then another minister might require something totally different.

For example, I have found that when certain ministers are laying hands on the sick, they often want music to help them. Some ministers I work with want the music upbeat and moving, while others want it slow and more reverent. Which is right? Both are right. Whatever will help them to minister is the right thing to do.

Sometimes they will say to the worship leader, "Do whatever you have on your heart to do." What should he do then? Whatever he has on his heart to do! God is not in a box, but many times we are. That doesn't mean anyone is wrong. The worship leader just has to find a way to help the ministers and do it the best that he can.

INSTANT IN SEASON AND OUT

It is difficult to do something we aren't used to, especially in front of an audience. That's why it is good for us to be instant in season and out, like it says in 2 Timothy 4:2. We should be ready for anything that might happen in a service.

Several years ago, a friend and I decided to go to a Kenneth Copeland meeting in Little Rock, Arkansas. I had met Kenneth before, but I didn't think he would remember me.

Kenneth had been preaching for a couple hours and finally said, "Let's all stand." I was thrilled. I immediately got up and was looking for the quickest way out of the building. I wanted to get to the car before everyone else did and head toward a restaurant.

Right then Kenneth said, "RayGene, come on up here and give that out."

I couldn't believe my ears. Surely he didn't want me to tell what I was thinking! I must have turned white as a sheet. I started toward the stage, but was so flabbergasted that I couldn't even remember my name, much less be ready to flow with the Spirit. It seemed as if I walked for a mile, but I finally made it onto the stage.

I went up to Kenneth, and he was about to hand me the microphone when suddenly he pulled it back and began prophesying to me. The Lord was speaking through Kenneth, giving me instructions about what I was supposed to do. I didn't hear a word that was said. I had to get a tape of the prophecy and listen to it later. But what was said came to pass just as it had been spoken.

Everything turned out great, but I had a talk with the Lord about it later. Our conversation went something like this:

"Why did You do that to me?" I asked.

He had a good response. He said, "If you had been paying attention to the Holy Ghost's prompting on the inside of you, you would have been ready."

God bailed me out anyway, but from then on, I have done my best to go to a meeting ready for anything. I strive to be instant in season and out. These are the last days, and we never know what's going to happen!

PRAISE SONGS OR WORSHIP SONGS

I have heard many different definitions people have for praise songs and worship songs. The general consensus is that people think of "praise" as the fast songs we do first and "worship" as the slow songs we do last. Personally, I have found it quite difficult to separate the two.

The truth is, *tempo has nothing in the world to do with either praise or worship.*

We often think the praise songs get people warmed up and the worship songs bring in God's glory. But I have seen His glory come into the room just as much, if not more so in some cases, when people are shouting, dancing and running around the room! During times like this, I have seen people's lives changed right before my eyes. People have been ministering to the Lord, with tears running down their faces. I have also seen times when people had the same results during quiet times, when we were singing softly to the Lord.

Remember, there are no formulas today. The key for us as New Testament believers is being led by the Spirit of God. We don't always know what people need, but God does. If we follow Him, He will get us exactly where we need to be, exactly how we need to get there.

PREFERENCES

One night after I had sung in a large convention, a minister came to me and said, "Now those songs you did

tonight are what *we* like. That's *our* favorite kind of music."
I had sung a few ballads that night because I felt led to go in
that direction. What he meant was he didn't like the more
upbeat songs.

I thought to myself that we shouldn't have a favorite style
when it comes to a service. *Our* favorite should be whatever
God wants to do through us.

Now if you are listening to music in your car or at home,
then you can listen to whatever you want. But when we come
together in a meeting, we should be praying for God to do
what *He* wants to do. He knows the people who are there. He
knows what they need and how to reach them. We can't be
letting our preferences get involved.

GET OUT OF THE RUT

I think it would be good in some cases to do slower songs
first, then do more upbeat songs before we turn it over to
whoever is next. Or just do *all* slow songs or *all* fast songs.

The point is, let's not just do things a certain way because
everyone else does it that way. Let's *not get in a rut* with how we
do things.

Actually, after talking to many ministers, I have found that
some would rather be handed a service after people are up
rejoicing. Many times the people are more alert and sharper
than they are after twenty minutes or so of "so-called"
worship, and it's easier to preach or teach them.

This leads me to the next point: What is the purpose of the
meeting?

WHAT'S YOUR PURPOSE?

Most people conduct every meeting *exactly* the same. Now

if they are having a regular weekly service, and they know how they want things to be and what works best for them, that's great. But many people will have a guest minister in and still do the same things they usually do.

It would be more beneficial for people to ask guest ministers what they want and how they want the service handed over to them. Also, the people should be conscious of the fact that they have a guest. They shouldn't be taking an hour for praise and worship, or anything else for that matter, before giving control of the service over to their guest. What is the purpose of the meeting? If they have invited someone to come and minister, then that person should be allowed to do so.

HONOR YOUR GUESTS

When I did a meeting myself in another country, they sang for over an hour before they gave me the service. They left me about twenty-five minutes to minister after I had flown halfway around the world!

The worship leader said it was hard to stop, that there was such a strong anointing on the music, much stronger than usual. They never thought that maybe the reason the anointing was so strong on the music was because that was how I was going to minister there. You might be surprised how many places that has happened.

While working with other ministers in meetings, I have seen the same thing happen to them.

One particular minister I work with frequently is a great evangelist and soulwinner. I can't tell you how many times people will get up before they hand the service over to him and give an altar call. They even say, "There is such an anointing here to get people saved." It's true; there *is* an anointing there to get people saved — *that evangelist's anointing!* But they must let him flow in it. That's why he came there!

I have also seen it happen with people who have a healing ministry. Before the service is turned over to the minister with the anointing to do it, people will start flowing in that healing anointing. Many times they say, "This is unusual for me; I never do this." The reason they don't is because the minister who is anointed to flow like that usually isn't there for them to be able to flow in that anointing.

GOD WILL SHOW YOU THINGS TO COME

Many people think if they get something from the Spirit of God, surely they are supposed to act on it. But that is not necessarily the case.

Many times God is just leading us by His Spirit, and if we are in tune, we will sense what is happening in the Spirit realm. I believe that is what occurred in the two examples just given: when they give the altar call before the evangelist gets up to minister and when they start flowing in the healing anointing before turning over the service to the minister with that anointing.

God may be showing you things to come, but that doesn't mean you are the one who is supposed to do it. Be sensitive not only to know *what* is going on, but to see *who* God wants to use.

PSALMS, HYMNS AND SPIRITUAL SONGS

A worship leader should flow in and out of prophecy. Psalms, hymns and spiritual songs are a part of that, but acting on it doesn't make the worship leader a prophet.

Actually, *every* believer should be operating in this aspect of worship and praise, not just the worship leaders or psalmists. Look at what 1 Corinthians 14:26 says, with italics added for emphasis:

> **How is it then, brethren? when ye come together, *every one of you* hath a psalm, hath a doctrine, hath a tongue, hath a revelation, hath an interpretation. Let all things be done unto edifying.**

This ability is for *all* of us!

THE ACTS OF THE HOLY GHOST

It can be so fulfilling when you see God's presence come in the room and you realize you can create an avenue for Him to come down. He is always with us; He lives on the inside of us. But there is not just the Spirit *within*, there is the Spirit *upon*!

As we said earlier, the Spirit of God falls today just like He did in the book of Acts. As a matter of fact, we are still living in the book of Acts. It's the only book in the Bible that has not been completed. In most Bibles it is titled The Acts of the Apostles. However, Stephen and Philip weren't apostles, so it is not just acts of the apostles. It really should be thought of as the acts of the Holy Ghost through the Church! Thank God, the Church is still alive and well, and the Holy Ghost is still active!

In the book, *John G. Lake — His Life, His Sermons, His Boldness of Faith*, it tells of a vision he had in 1920. In this vision, an angel appeared and opened a Bible to the book of Acts, drawing Lake's attention to the outpouring of the Spirit on Pentecost and to the entire book of Acts itself. Then the angel said to him:

This is Pentecost as God gave it through the heart of Jesus. Strive for this. Contend for this. Teach the people to pray for this. For this alone will meet the necessity of the human heart and have the power to overcome the forces of darkness.

CONCLUSION

CONCLUSION

Many of the views in this writing may seem strict to some people; however, I believe if we are going to have God's presence visit us in the way we know He desires, we need to welcome Him in our midst. We can only do that by following the Word and the Spirit. God does not inhabit our ideas of what praise is; He inhabits what the Bible says praise is.

This book is designed simply to help bring God's people some definition on the subject. It covers what I believe are the most crucial subjects and Scriptures on New Testament Praise and Worship. Some of the content may cover things you have never heard anyone address before, or aren't sure about. I urge you to do as Second Timothy 2:15 says, **Study to show thyself approved unto God, a workman that needeth not to be ashamed, rightly dividing the word of truth.**

If the Word can be rightly divided, it can be wrongly divided. There are lots of people with sincere hearts who may be doing things that do not line up with the Word of God. This is not to bring condemnation or judgment on anyone, but simply to help anyone who wants to be helped further understand the subject. In this book I gave examples of where I was wrong myself and made adjustments to line up with the Word of God.

Always put the Word of God first — before your favorite preacher, before your own personal preferences. Heaven and earth will pass away, but the Word of God will stand forever.

ENDNOTES

CHAPTER 1

[1]Finis Jennings Dake, "New Testament Section," in *The Dake Annotated Reference Bible* (Lawrenceville: Dake Bible Sales, Inc.), John 4:27, p. 97, A.

CHAPTER 2

[1]W. E. Vine, Merrill F. Unger, William White, Jr. *Vine's Complete Expository Dictionary of Old and New Testament Words.* (Nashville: Thomas Nelson, 1985), p. 236, "pleroo."

CHAPTER 3

[1]Source of article unknown.

[2]Kenneth E. Hagin, *Plans, Purposes, and Pursuits* (Tulsa: RHEMA Bible Church, 1988), 96.

CHAPTER 4

[1]Vine, p. 185.

CHAPTER 5

[1]James H. Strong. *Strong's Exhaustive Concordance.* Compact Ed. (Grand Rapids: Baker, 1992), "Hebrew and Chaldee Dictionary," p. 47, #3034.

[2]Strong, "Greek Dictionary of the New Testament," p. 30, #1867.

ABOUT THE AUTHOR

RayGene Wilson is an anointed minister who is recognized as one who will boldly preach and sing the uncompromised Word of God. He has been in full-time ministry since 1979 and is a licensed minister with Kenneth Copeland Ministries. He has ministered with various music ministries over the years and has appeared on every major Christian Television program in America. RayGene traveled full time with Kenneth Hagin for several years and ministers in all of Kenneth Copeland's Believers Conventions. He has recorded many albums, including four solo albums to date, and is signed to KCP records.

In 1991 he married Beth Hogue from Nashville, Tennessee. Beth is also a licensed minister and is a graduate of The University of Mississippi, Rhema Bible Training Center, and Victory Bible Training Center in Nashville. Together they travel around the world taking God's Word and the move of the Holy Ghost to the nations.

To contact RayGene Wilson,
write:
RayGene Wilson Ministries
P. O. Box 4779
Tulsa, OK 74159
*Please include your prayer requests and comments
when you write.*

Copies of this book are available
from your local bookstore.

Harrison House
Tulsa, Oklahoma 74153

In Canada contact:
Word Alive
P. O. Box 670
Niverville, Manitoba
CANADA ROA 1E0

The Harrison House Vision

Proclaiming the truth and the power
Of the Gospel of Jesus Christ
With excellence;

Challenging Christians to
Live victoriously,
Grow spiritually,
Know God intimately.